This book is dedicated to

Bubbles the Basset

Will McNeil is an artist, and architectural designer from Oak Park, IL. His art has been featured in several art exhibitions, including one solo exhibition, and he has sold his art to no less than half a dozen people. He has also worked as a designer for both commercial and residential architecture. With the help of Avery's eye for detail and extensive alcohol collection, has become a cocktail king.

Avery Campbell is a photographer and chronic hobby-collector from Chicago, IL. His photography has been featured on several fridges, including his own and his grandma's, and has done documentation for a number of artists/galleries as well as a renowned Midwestern auction house. With the help of Will's fearless attitude and adventurous palate, he too has become a cocktail king.

INTRODUCTION

A few years back, Avery and Will simultaneously and independently found and fell in love with the album "Paraiso." They had been tossing around the idea of making a cocktail book for a while, but when that happened, they knew what they had to do. Nine cocktails inspired by and named after the songs of the 1979 album. Their mission was to create imagery to evoke the feeling and the spirit of the drinks, using photographs and drawings by Avery and Will, respectively. They paired these images with short passages that aim to convey the atmosphere. And for those who would like a deeper understanding of the source material, the English translations of the original song lyrics have been provided alongside every recipe.

The logical interpretation of this book is to listen through the whole album in one sitting, drinking each cocktail in conjunction with the song of the same name, alone or with friends, and with no distractions. This, however, is ill-advised as that would be a dangerous amount of alcohol. So, in the case that one manages to source all of these ingredients and wants to try it, please scale down the drinks to a fraction of the size. Now without further ado, enjoy this Experimental, Multi-Sensory, Cocktail Journey, shepherded by the Jazz-techno-exotica fusion soundscape that is… "Paraiso."

TOKIO RUSH
東京ラッシュ

Ingredients:
1/4 oz Crème de Cassis
1/4 oz Maraschino Liqueur
1 oz Passion Fruit Juice
2 1/2 oz Milkis
1 Dash Orange Bitters

Directions:
1. Fill shaker with ice.
2. Add bitters, Maraschino, and Cassis to shaker and shake.
3. Strain into a Collins glass and top with with Milkis, leaving some room at the top for passion fruit juice.
4. Float a generous splash of passion fruit juice.

The last train has departed, but the night has just begun! Flashing signs fight for your attention, the warm glow of incandescent bulbs spill out from the row of local bars. "Irasshaimase!" A man behind a bar, dressed in full clown attire, invites you inside. As you wriggle your way into the last seat, he hands you a bowl of passion fruit. "Juice, please!"

From that way and this way squeeze squeeze
The intersection all year round squeeze squeeze
    TOKIO RUSH   Rush from place to place
    TOKIO RUSH   Life's a gas gas gas
    TOKIO RUSH   A trip to Honolulu would be so refreshing

TWIST! TWIST! Speed along the winding highway
TWIST! TWIST! So contrary
    TOKIO RUSH   Rush from place to place
    TOKIO RUSH   Life's a gas gas gas
    TOKIO RUSH   Ah, woo ...

From Moscow, from Dhaka squeeze squeeze
The control tower all year round squeeze squeeze
    TOKIO RUSH   Bursting with information rush
    TOKIO RUSH   Spies with intelligence rush
    TOKIO RUSH   Escape to Hong Kong in a rush

More and more such a heavy feeling
But then again such a foolish feeling
    TOKIO RUSH   Rush from place to place
    TOKIO RUSH   Life's a gas gas gas
    TOKIO RUSH   Ah, woo ...

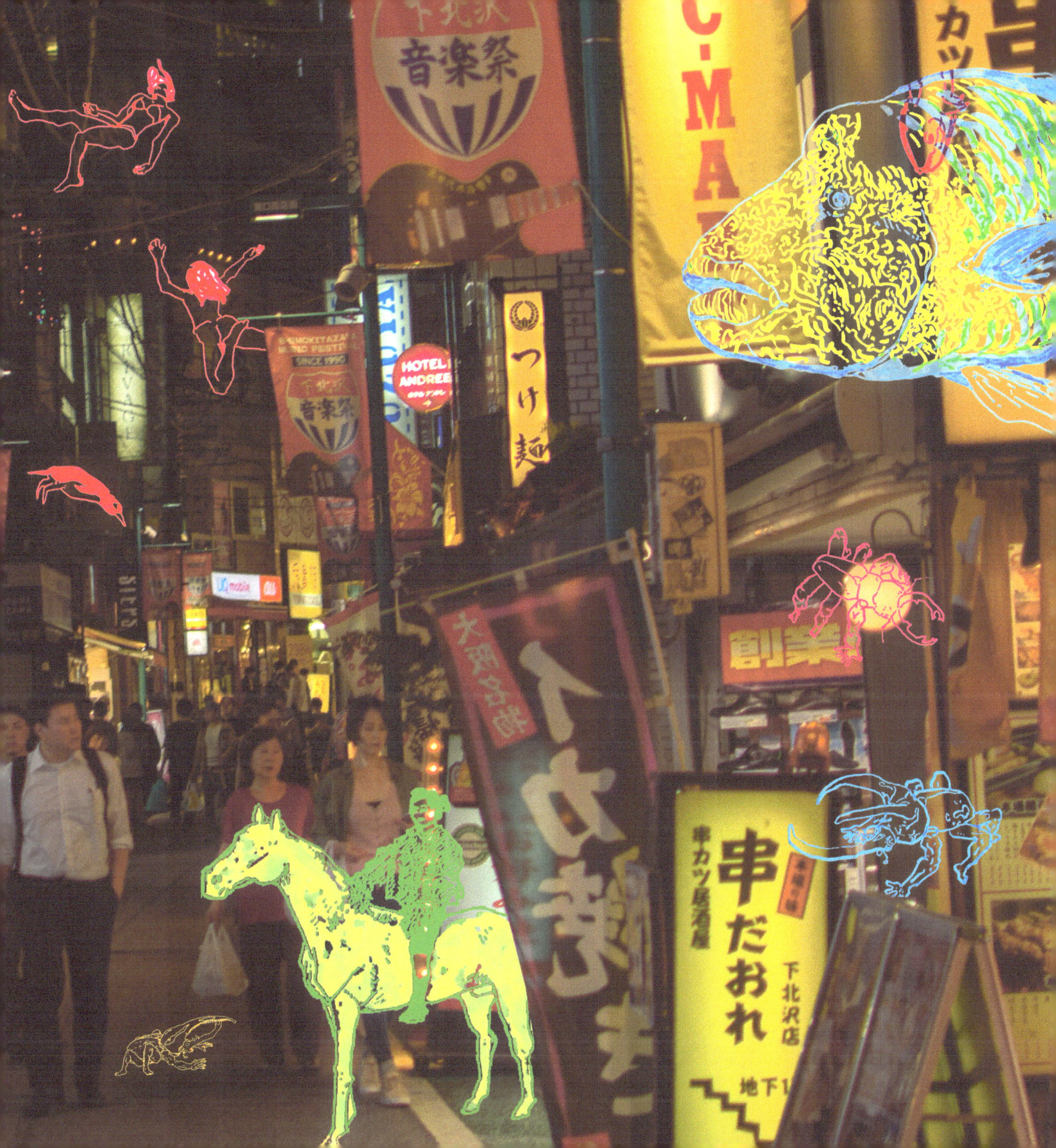

下北沢
音楽祭
C-MA
カツ
つけ麺
HOTEL
ANDREE
SHIMOKITAZAWA
MUSIC FESTIVAL
SINCE 1990
音楽祭
割烹
串カツ居酒屋
串
だ
お
れ
下北沢店
地下1

SHIMENDOKA

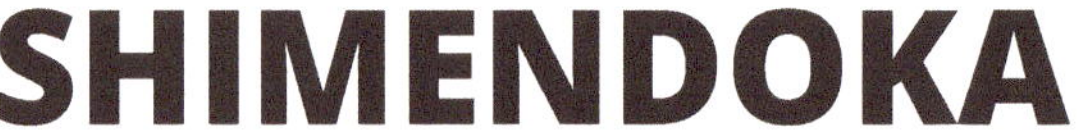

<table>
<tr><td>

Ingredients:
3/4 oz Rum
3/4 oz Campari
3/4 oz Orange Curacao
3/4 oz Dry Vermouth

</td><td>

Directions:
1. Fill mixing glass with ice
2. Add all ingredients and stir
3. Strain into rocks glass with ice
4. Garnish with orange peel

</td></tr>
</table>

Just four equal parts.

North, South, East, West, together.

Liquid harmony.

<Spring Flowers>
    I will go when morning breaks
    From the western door
    To ancient India where the lotus flowers bloom
    To meet the god almighty
    *Beyond the flowers and the storms I will be going
    Shake off all the sad words I will be going

<Summer Wind>
    I will go when the flowers bloom
    To the southern seas
    Where the warm wind blows
    And bathe in the Caribbean sun
    *Chorus
    Get out of the way you devil, you're in the way

<Autumn Moon>
    I will go when the wind blows
    From the eastern skies
    To Chaldea, the Land of Magicians
    And bathe in the moonlight
    *Chorus

<Northern Bird>
    I will go when the sun goes down
    To the northern island
    Chasing the firebird
    That I once saw in your town
    Be careful when you catch that creature
    The flames will scorch you and burn you to ashes
    Get out of the way you devil, you're in the way

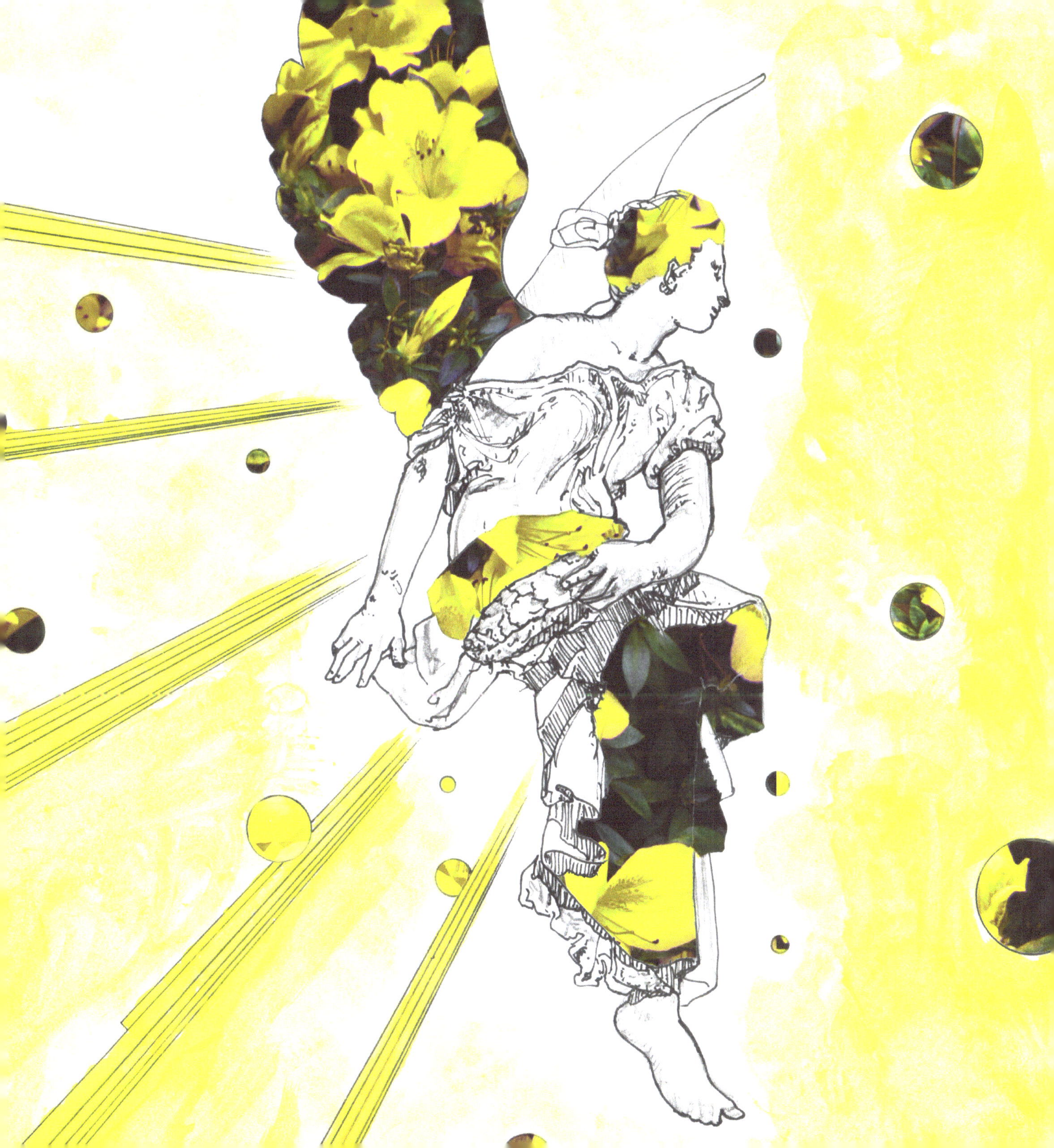

JAPANESE RHUMBA
ジャパニーズ・ルンバ

Ingredients:
1 1/2 oz Cachaca
1/4 oz Triple Sec
1/4 oz Blue Curacao
1/4 oz Yuzu Juice
1/2 Starfruit
Carbonated Aloe Juice*

Directions:
1. Muddle starfruit in shaker
2. Add ice and all ingredients besides aloe juice
3. Strain into coupe and float a pour of carbonated aloe juice
4. Garnish with starfruit slice

A chameleon gives you a kiss. Your eyes open. Time to stretch.

A soapy sphere shines in the sun. Your lips pucker. Time to stroll.

A starry blanket lifts you into the cosmos. Your eyes shut. Time to luau.

Doko iku no koko irasshaine
Chotto anone ohayo gozaimasu

*Japanese rhumba ay yai yai
Japanese rhumba ay yai
Japanese rhumba ay yai yai
Ohayo gozaimasu

Nani mama san hayaku papa san hai
Ano ojosan chotto matte kudasai
*Ref.
Chotto matte kudasai

Nani ano ne sutekine kesho hai
Nani yaru no ano konnichiwa
*Ref.
Ano konnichiwa

Konbanwa banwa
Konbanwa banwa
Konbanwa banwa
Oyasuminasai

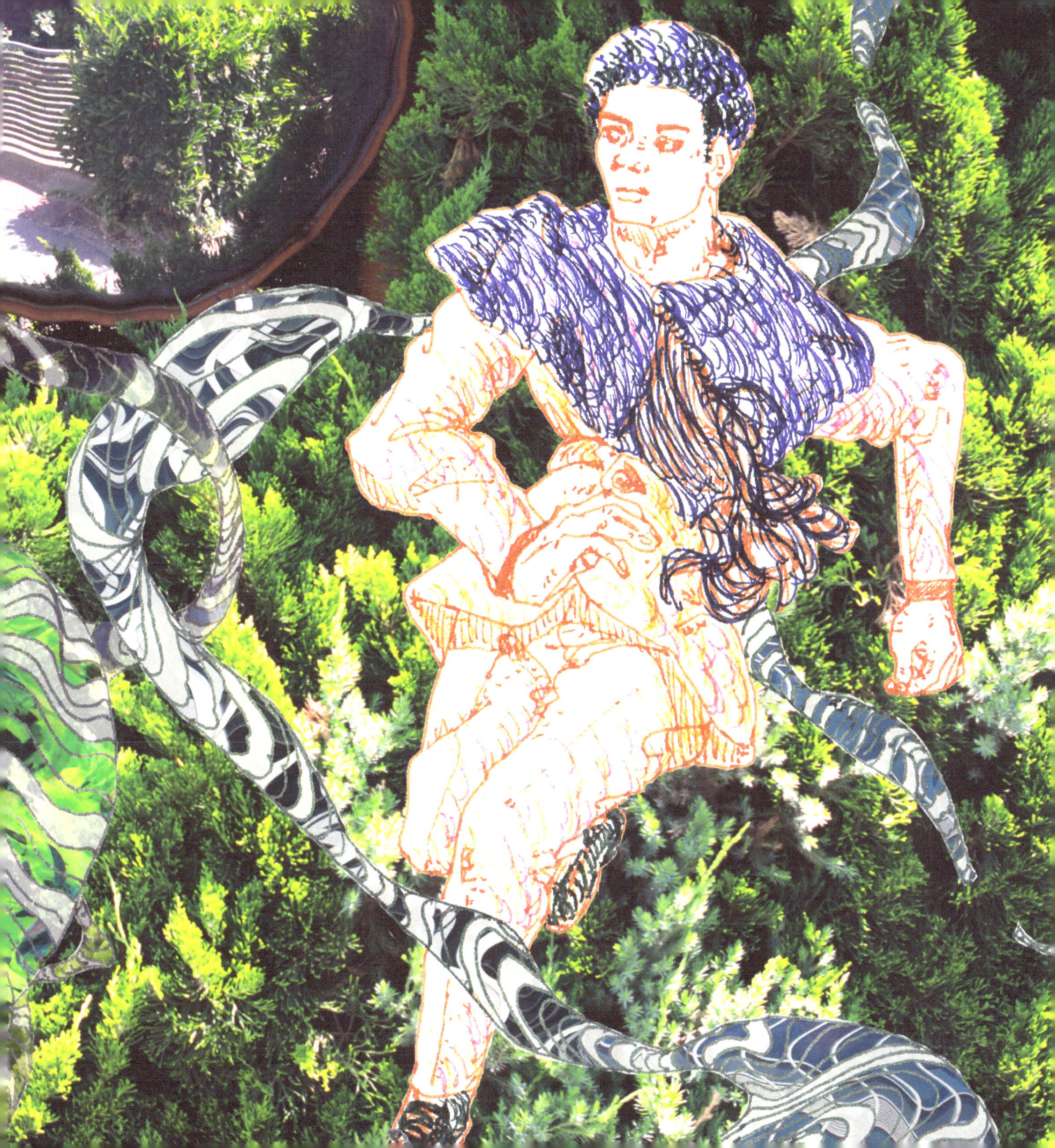

ASATOYA YUNTA
安里屋ユンタ

Ingredients:
Beer (whatever you've got)
Sake (any)
Pickled Ginger Juice
Somethin' Special

Directions:
1. Get your favorite glass or mug
2. Pour a lot of beer
3. Pour some sake
4. Pour a splash of juice from a jar of pickled ginger
5. Add Somethin' Special. Will recommends apricot juice. Avery prefers soy sauce. Get wild!

You sit on the porch as a sun-bleached hand offers you a glass.

"What's in this?!" you ask,

"Whatever you like…"

You're like a thorny flower from the fields (saa yui yui)
Keeping me from going home when the sun sets
    Mata haarinu tsundara kanushamayo

Happy and shy that rumors are spreading (saa yui yui)
Like white lilies you can't stand still
    Mata haarinu tsundara kanushamayo

Kuyama Asatoya
You were born so beautiful
    Mata haarinu tsundara kanushamayo

So pretty since the day you were born (saa yui yui)
So pale since you were so small
    Mata haarinu tsundara kanushamayo

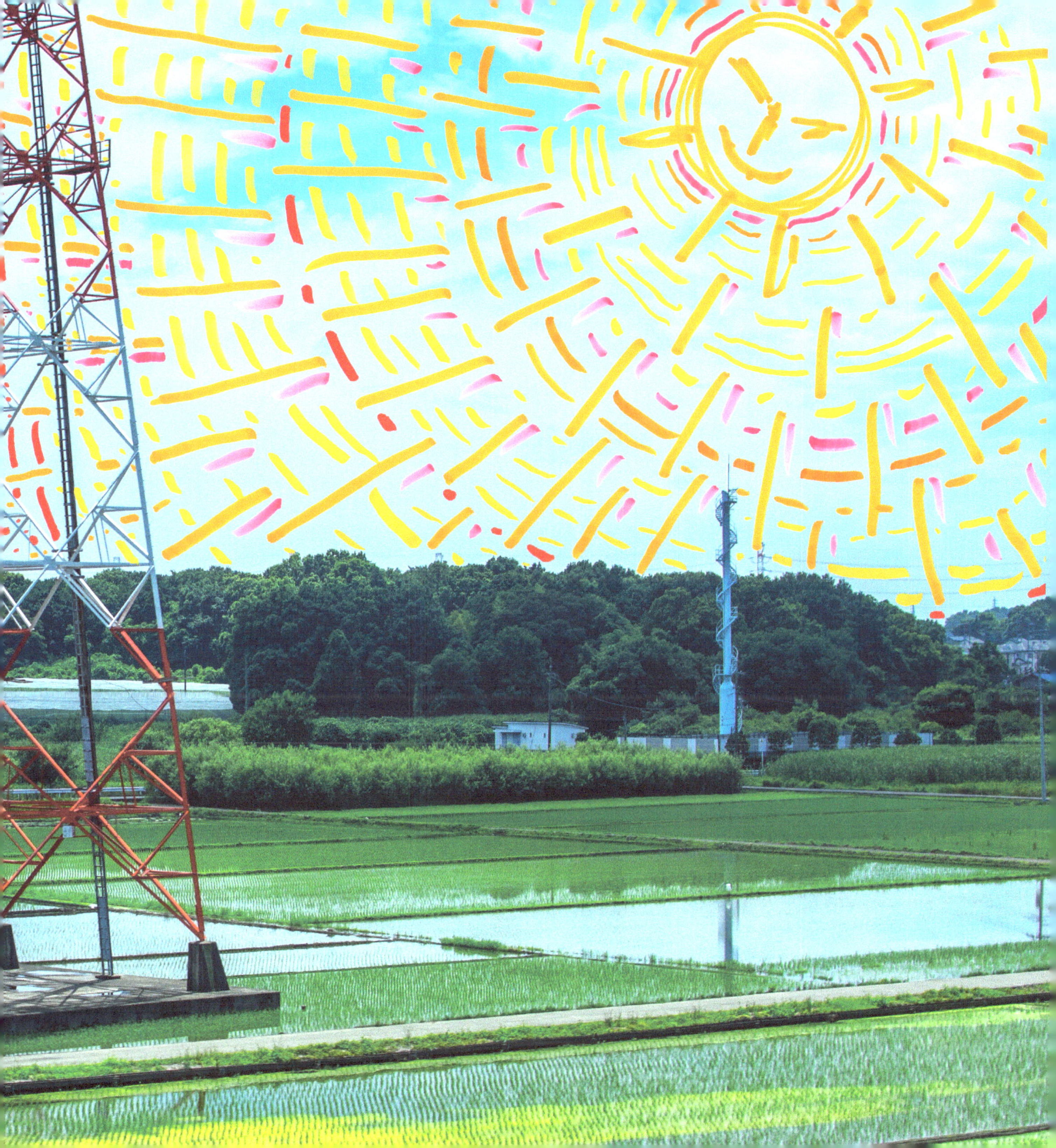

FUJIYAMA MAMA
フジヤマ・ママ

Ingredients:
2 oz Sake (Ginjo-style)
1/2 oz Ancho Reyes Chile Liqueur
1/4 oz Cinnamon Turbinado
    Simple Syrup*
1/4 oz Yuzu Juice
1-2 dashes Togarashi
1-2 dashes Denman Bitters*

Directions:
1. Fill shaker with ice
2. Add all ingredients then shake
3. Strain into coupe
4. Garnish with a slice of jalapeno

You notice the bounce of his pompadour as he takes his seat. Eating in silence, the flame of his lighter awakens the red eye at the end of his cigarette. From his chest pocket appears a hamster, sporting some suave shades. Mirroring the man's movements, lighting up a comically small cigarette. Rad…

You've been to Nagasaki, Hiroshima too
The things you did to them
Baby, you kin do to me

*'Cause you're a Fujiyama Mama
And you're just about to blow your top
Fujiyama, yama, Fujiyama
And when you start eruptin'
Ain't nobody gonna make you stop

You drink a quart of SAKE, smoke dynamite
You chased it with tobacy
An' then shoot out the light
*Ref.

I'm an attraction Fujiyama Mama
Hot lava hidden beneath my snow white skin
Think about it Fujiyama Mama, yama, Fujiyama
Burning up and erupting like a volcano

Well I can say you're crazy, so deaf an' dumb
But you can cause destruction
Just like the atom bomb
*Ref.

You drink a quart of sake, smoke dynamite
You chased it with tobacy
An' then shoot out the lights
*Ref.

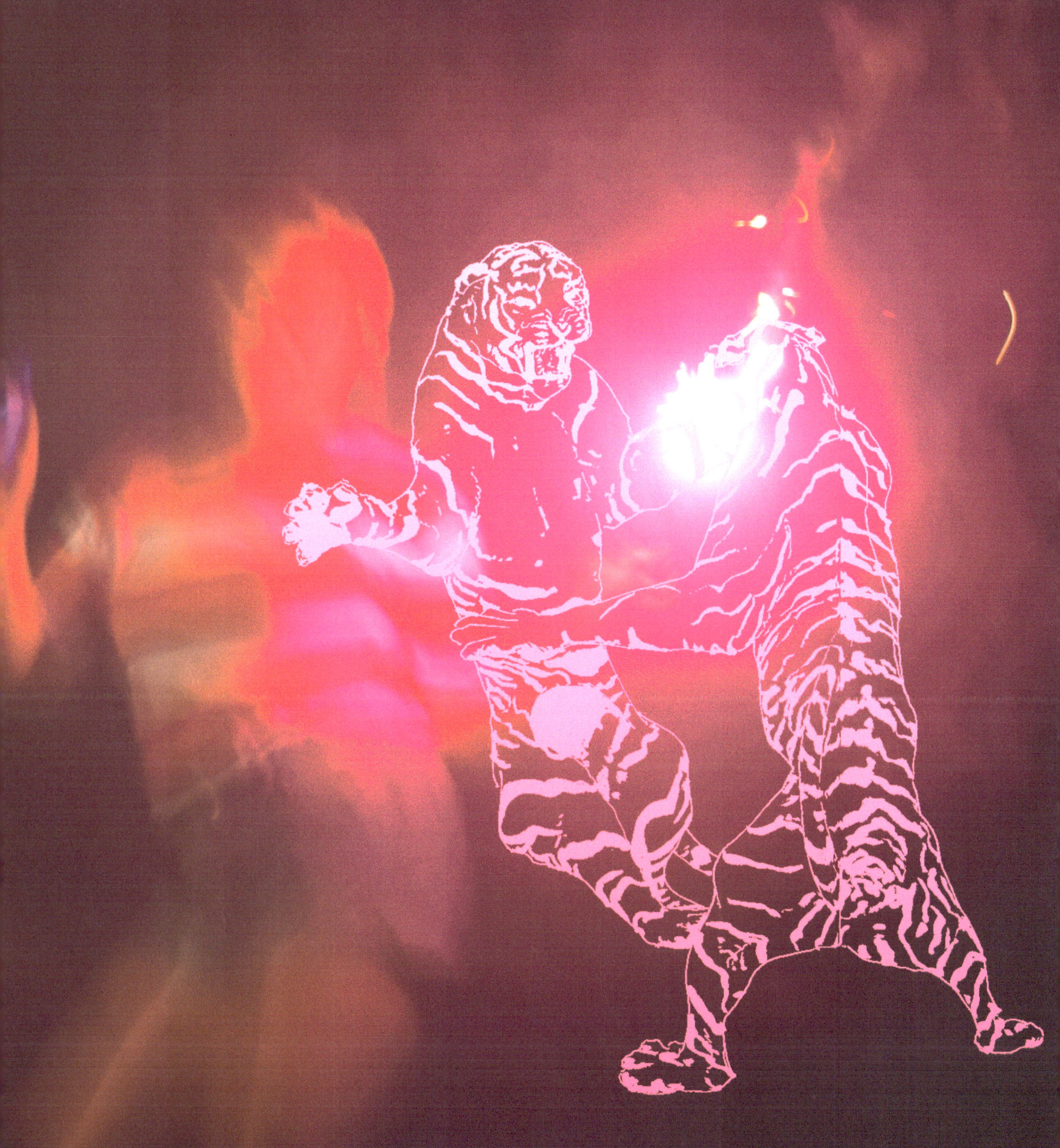

FEMME FATALE

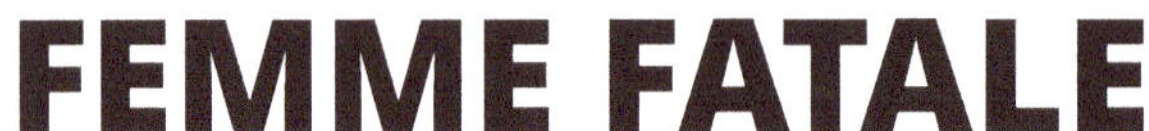

ファム・ファタール〜妖婦

Ingredients:
1 1/4 oz Gin
1/2 oz Midori
3/4 oz Dry Sherry
1/2 oz Egg White

Directions:
1. Shake egg white without ice (one min.)
2. Add ice and all ingredients then shake
3. Strain into coupe
4. Garnish with a slice of kiwi

A shimmer of light breaks through the fog, just catching your eye. Water up to your waist, you advance methodically. Faint silhouettes are slowly unveiled. You arrive at the bank of mangroves where you encounter two young crocodiles seated for a lovely candlelit dinner. You give a nod and continue on through the mist.

This is the edge of the world
Mysterious oasis hidden in the city
My search for you continues
And when I find you
The birds will holler beneath the crimson sky

When the sun sets in the west
And the moon rises to illuminate the darkness
From the moon burnt skin faintly arises
The scent of blood, sweat and tears
A sign of death

*Listen, you can hear it
The rumbling of the earth
It echoes in the distance, it vibrates
It's a premonition
Make it go away, femme fatale!

You're the devil's daughter
And once again I'm a captive
Tonight when the moon is full
The god of fear will swoop down
And take you away
*Ref.

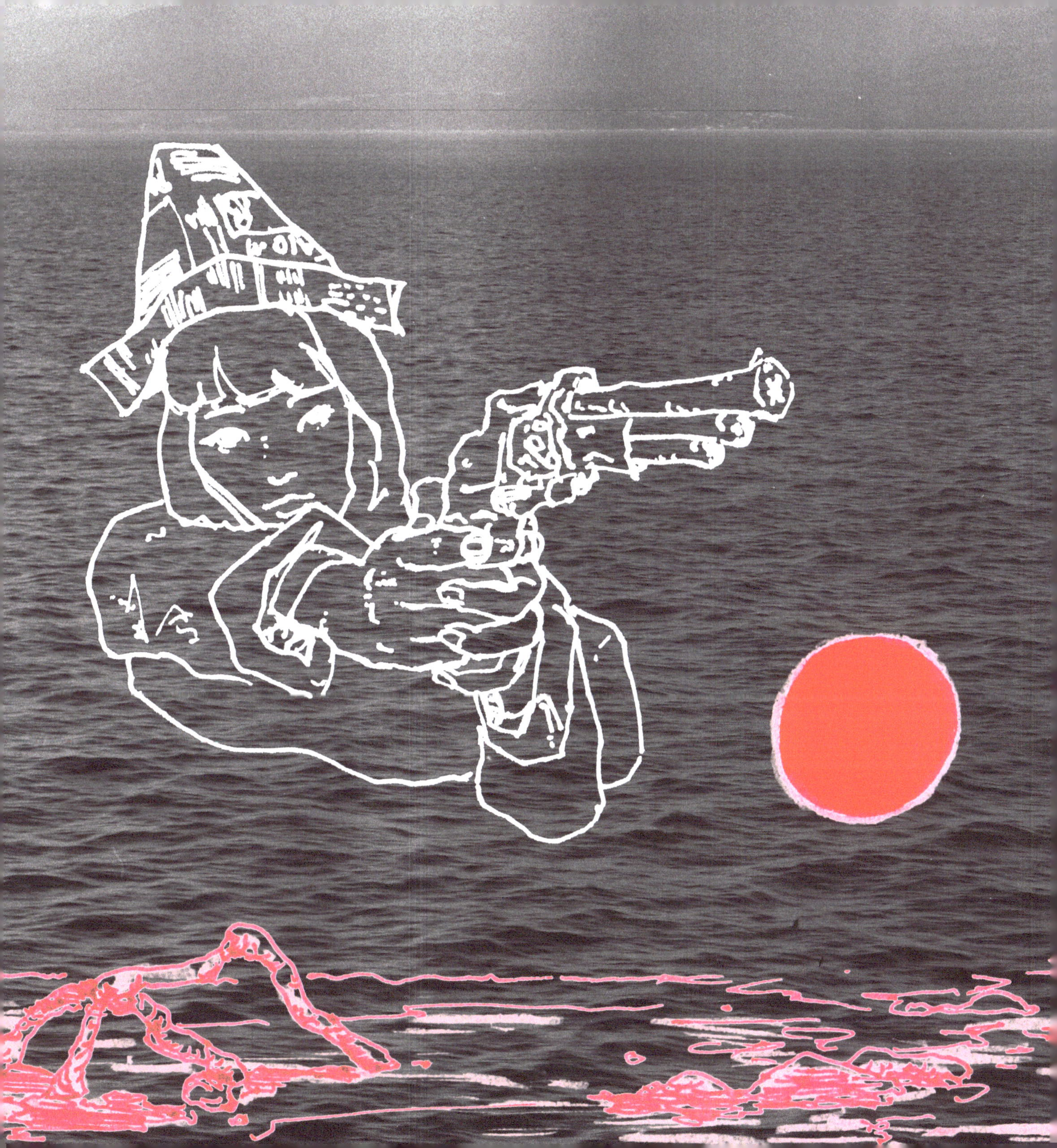

SHAMBALA SIGNAL
シャンバラ通信

Ingredients:
2 oz Gin (pref. Spruce-influenced)
3/4 oz Crème de Violette
1/4 oz Lillet

Directions:
1. Fill mixing glass with ice
2. Add all ingredients and stir
3. Strain into cocktail glass

Primordial Emotion   Mind Untraceable   Vanishing Self   Viscous Psyche

Embrace Fear   Material Tranquility   Transcend Control

Become Sand

$$N = R_{+}f_{p}n_{e}f_{i}f_{j}f_{e}L$$

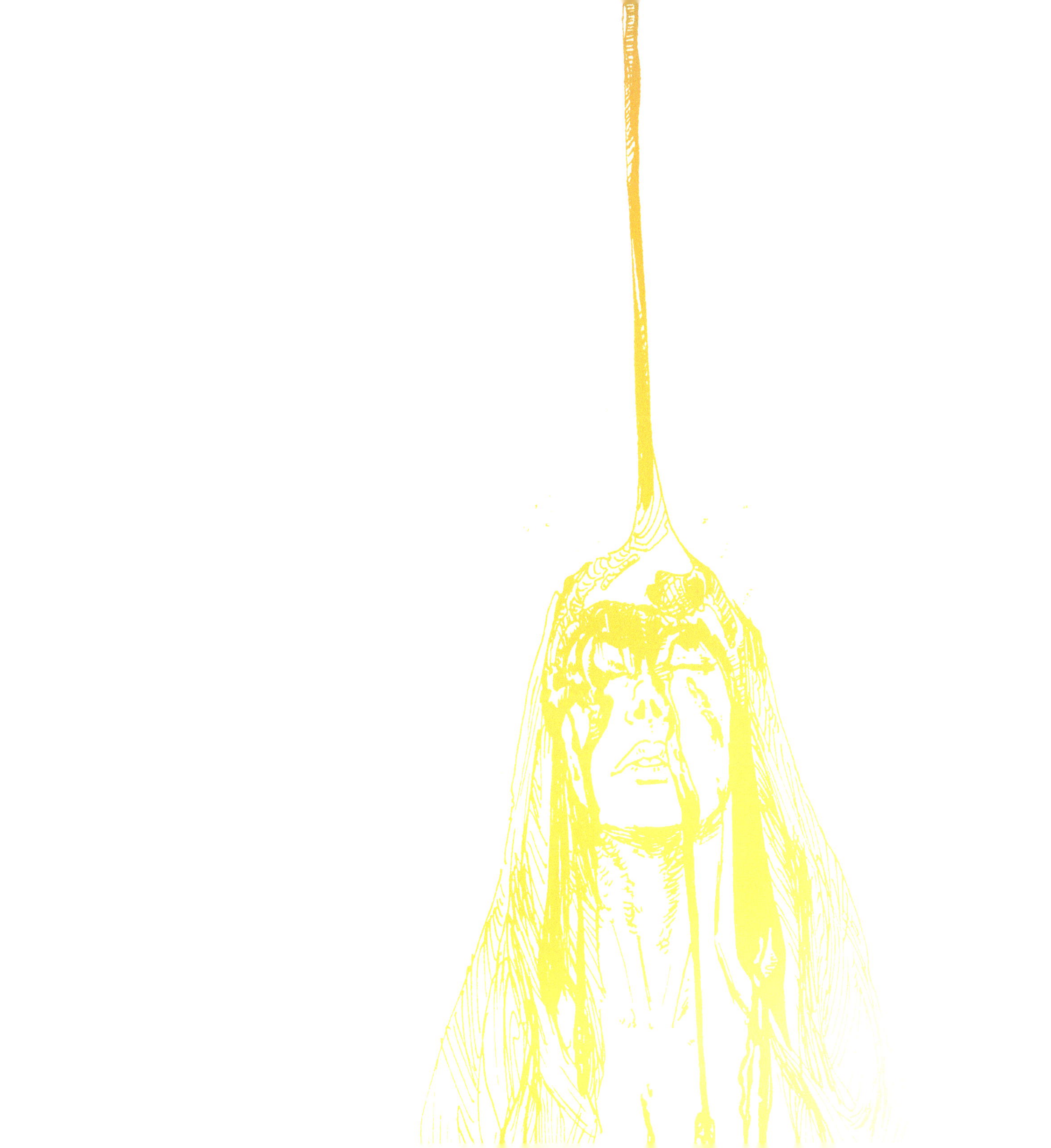

WORRY BEADS
ウォリー・ビーズ

Ingredients:
2 oz Shochu (pref. Barley-based)
1 oz Heavy Cream
1/2 oz Coffee Liqueur
1 dash Sesame Tincture*
1 dash Chocolate Bitters

Directions:
1. Fill shaker with ice
2. Add all ingredients then shake
3. Strain into rocks glass with ice
4. Garnish with an orange peel

The old man walks down the boardwalk in his patchwork jacket, placing bottles of milk every four paces. He sits at the end with a milk of his own, watching as, one by one, the bottles are plucked off the sea-stained planks by thirsty fish.

---

*Let's go back, back to the desert moon
Plant in your heart a seed of the moon

    A hundred and eight kinds of worries
    Just count them one by one
    See, your body feels lighter
    You can go anywhere
    Right now

*Ref.
Count-a WORRY BEADS
    Bathe in the moonlight, count the seeds and
    swallow your breath
    Look, the desert moon is expanding in your heart
    Right now

**Om Nama Chandraya
Shanti Shanti Chandraya

*Ref.
    The first one is for that one
    The second one is for this one
    See, it's all becoming untangled
    You can go anywhere
    Right now

**Ref.
    A hundred and eight kinds of worries
    Just teach them one by one

**Ref.
    Count-a WORRY BEADS

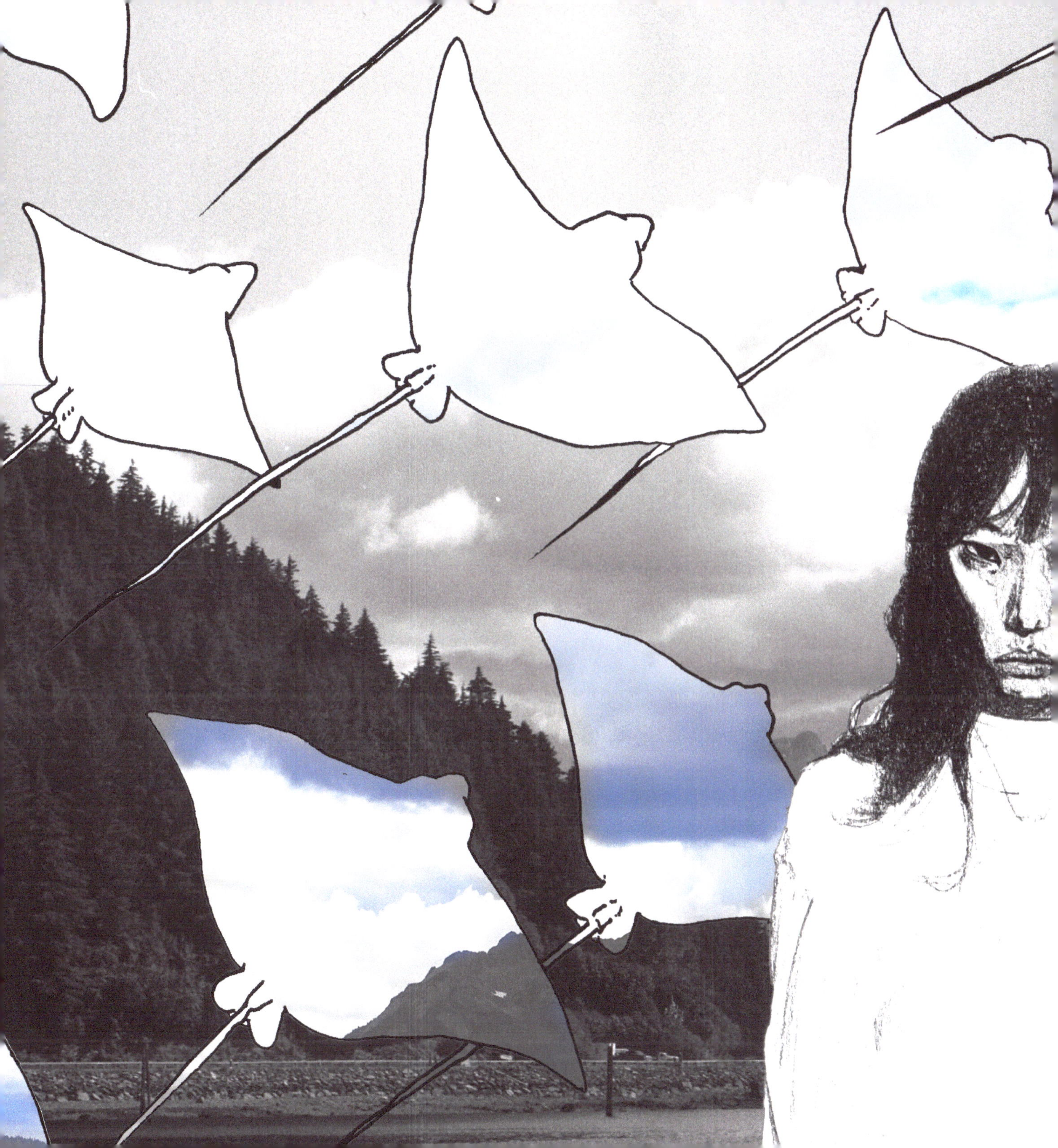

PARAISO
(BLUE ISLAND REDUX)

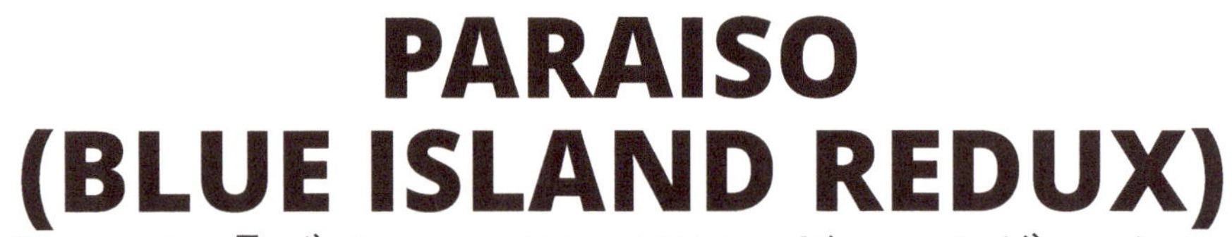

はらいそ「ブルー・アイランド・リダックス」

Ingredients:
1 1/2 oz Light Rum
3/4 oz Lime Juice
1/2 oz Blue Curacao
1/4 oz Simple Syrup
1 tsp Mint Tincture*
Soda Water

Directions:
1. Fill shaker with ice
2. Add all ingredients except soda water then shake
3. Strain into Collins glass with ice
4. Top with soda water
5. Garnish with pineapple and cherry

The dawn brings with it a new end.

The sun beams down upon you and yourself.

You stare at each other and smile.

That fantasy I once saw in a dream
Chasing it will take me to a place - a pier
Living here, it's a metropolis among cities
Even tomorrow, you can't escape from
this island nation

*From the pier
All aboard the ship from that strange land
Adios Farewell
To the city lights that looks like a woman
Kiss and say bye bye, good bye

Paradise ~ paraiso
Expand your fantasies
It's a mirage, paraiso
Melt away the reality

*Chorus

Someday the city and I will both become dusk
I will be near the who holds the key to love
Adios, farewell, sayonara

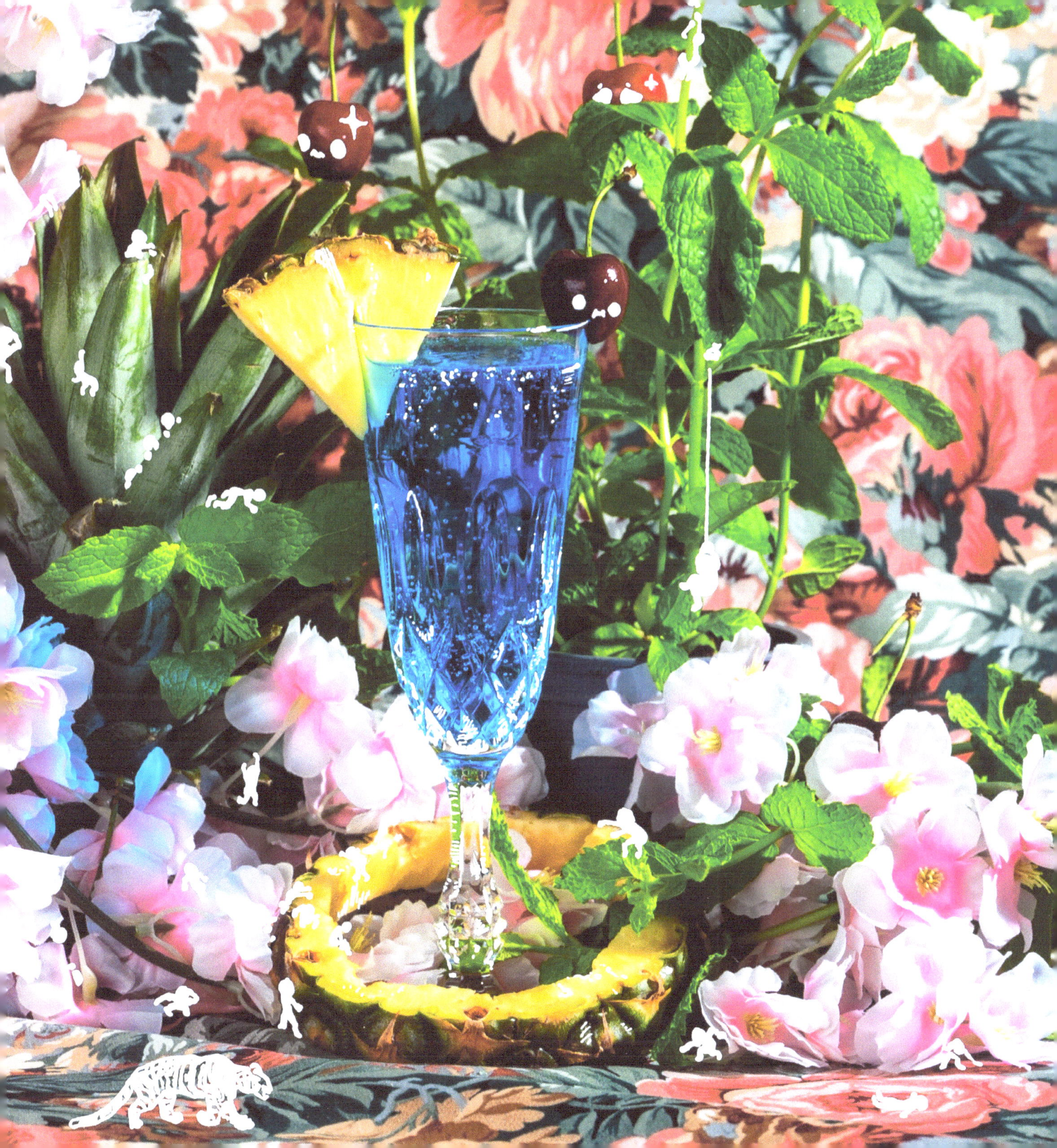

PARADISE LOST
(...and found)

The year is 1983. The House of Suntory is hosting their annual Suntory Tropical Cocktail Grand Prix. The newly crowned winner - the number one libation for transporting oneself to a distant tropical paradise - is the Blue Island! This drink, created by Hiroshi Yokoi, calls for Marine Club soda (in Blue Mint flavor, specifically). This was a short-lived soft drink, released by Suntory earlier that year.

Marine Club managed to gather a bit of hype amongst the public, from school-children passing around the rumor that the three flavors/colors (Blue Mint, Red Berry, and Green Lime) would become clear if you mixed the them all, to adults struck by a uniquely memorable commercial campaign featuring music by Malcolm McLaren, manager of the Sex Pistols.

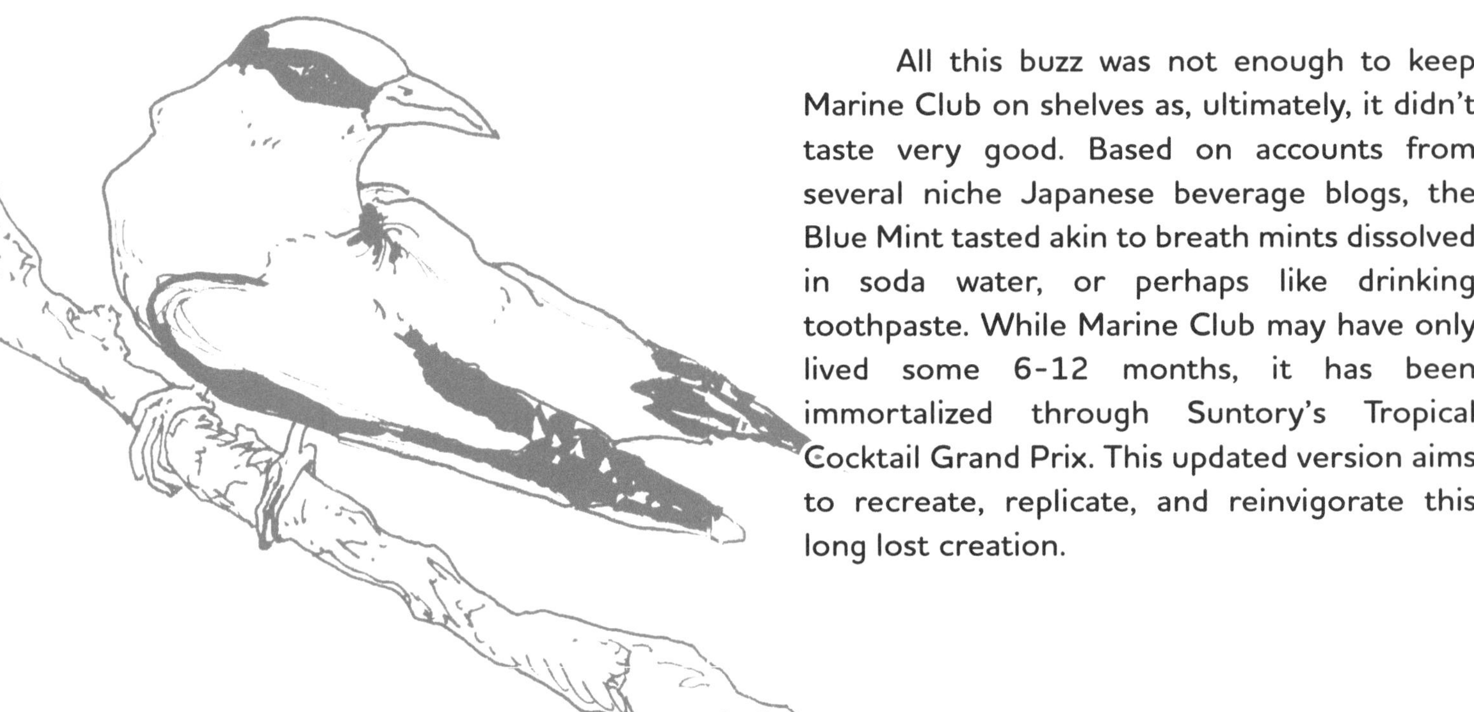

All this buzz was not enough to keep Marine Club on shelves as, ultimately, it didn't taste very good. Based on accounts from several niche Japanese beverage blogs, the Blue Mint tasted akin to breath mints dissolved in soda water, or perhaps like drinking toothpaste. While Marine Club may have only lived some 6-12 months, it has been immortalized through Suntory's Tropical Cocktail Grand Prix. This updated version aims to recreate, replicate, and reinvigorate this long lost creation.

GLOSSARY

Carbonated aloe juice — Bottles of aloe juice can be found at most Asian grocery stores, and at an increasing number of local grocery chains. Ideally, this juice should then be carbonated with a household soda-maker. For a simpler - albeit less flavorful - solution, mix equal parts aloe juice with soda water.

Cinnamon Turbinado simple syrup — Bring a cup of water to a boil. Pour in a cup of Turbinado sugar. Chuck a handful of cinnamon sticks in there. Stir until dissolved (the sugar, not the cinnamon sticks…)

Denman bitters — These cocktail bitters were a limited edition release by Bittered Sling. Good luck finding some! You are cordially invited to ponder the best possible substitution. These bitters are a bit pepper-y, with the addition of "Asian and sub-Gobi cultural spices".

Sesame tincture — Pour half a cup or so of sesame seeds into a cup of vodka, and let it infuse for about 48 hours. For better results, replace vodka with neutral grain spirits, such as Everclear. Experiment! White sesame or black sesame? Toasted or plain? Whole or ground? More or less?

Mint tincture — Get the vodka/neutral grain spirit back out. Drop a fistful of peppermint leaves and a fistful of spearmint leaves into a jar. Fresh is best, dried is fine. Cover with vodka and let steep for at least 48 hours.